Contemporary Crafts

Papier Mâché

Susanne Haines

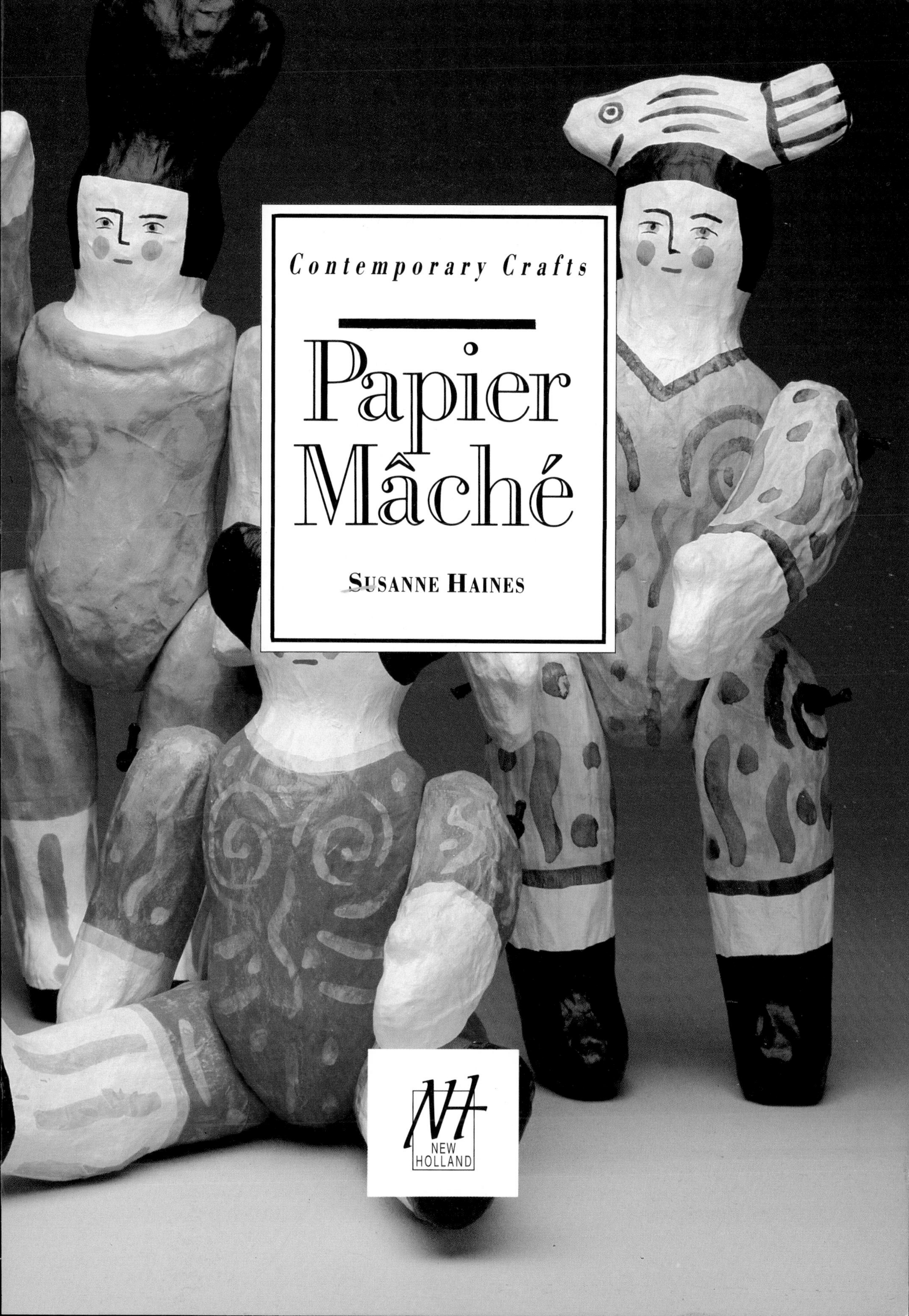

Contemporary Crafts

Papier Mâché

Susanne Haines

NH
NEW HOLLAND

This edition published in 1999 by
New Holland Publishers (UK) Ltd
London • Cape Town • Sydney • Auckland

24 Nutford Place
London W1H 6DQ
United Kingdom

80 McKenzie Street
Cape Town 8001
South Africa

3/2 Aquatic Drive
Frenchs Forest, NSW 2086
Australia

Unit 1A, 218 Lake Road
Northcote
Auckland
New Zealand

ISBN 1 85368 629 8

Printed and bound in Singapore by Tien Wah Press (Pte) Ltd

6 8 10 9 7 5

CONTENTS

INTRODUCTION

UNTIL RECENTLY, the term "papier mâché" (French for mashed paper) has evoked for many people dim recollections of childhood, of gluey fingers, schoolrooms strewn with newspapers and the creation of strange lumpy creatures. Today, however, the technique has been elevated to the status of a fresh and exciting craft and art form, rediscovered by artists eager to find a new creative means of expression for their work.

The craft of creating objects from layers of pasted paper, or from pulped paper has been known ever since waste paper has been available; and paper was invented in China in the second century AD. The diversity of its uses and qualities has appealed throughout history.

Papier mâché is inexpensive, remarkably lightweight and easy to handle, and ideal for making ephemeral objects from the very small to the very large: carnivals, festivals, theatres and circuses throughout the world have used papier mâché to create vast and extravagant temporary structures as well as masks.

The strength and durability of papier mâché is testified by the survival of Chinese warriors' masks, hardened with lacquer, dating from the second century AD. The technique of moulding pulp or paper sheets and glue, hardened by baking and finished with varnish or lacquer was known in France in the 17th century and subsequently in the rest of Europe.

. . . .

These highly decorative papier mâché vases by Marion Elliot demonstrate the use of bold and imaginative shapes, motifs and colour.

Methods of production were developed and refined to produce an extremely resilient material that reached its heyday in Europe and America in the second half of the 19th century. Its uses ranged from snuff boxes and calling card cases to furniture, architectural mouldings and coach panels. There are records of its use in the building of a boat, and, most extraordinary of all, for the construction of a prefabricated village ordered by an English immigrant to ease his settlement in Australia. The best-known papier mâché work surviving from this period are decorative objects and furniture with characteristic black lacquer finish and Oriental-inspired painting decorated with gold leaf and mother-of-pearl.

Papier mâché is chameleon-like in character, having the capability of imitating the visual appearance of other materials, such as wood, stone, clay or bronze. It can be worked roughly, emphasizing the nature of the material and the paper pieces, or it can be worked extremely finely to produce smooth surfaces and can be used to create highly intricate shapes on a miniature scale. These properties have been explored in the folk traditions throughout the world from the Americas to India and the Far East.

With mâché appearance is contradicted by reality. Although the eye may perceive an object made from papier mâché as substantial, when handled, its lightness never fails to surprise.

To those sensitive to its qualities, it has almost magical properties. It invites exploration of all its possibilities and gives free rein to expression. There are no restrictions, no rules, no prescribed traditions when dealing with this material.

The enjoyment of creating with papier mâché comes, too, from the different stages that must be worked, and seeing the piece slowly evolve. After the initial

idea comes the sculptural element, which may involve assembling a construction or framework or simply finding a suitable mould. Applying the layers of paper is time-consuming, but once you have developed a rhythm it can become quite mesmerizing and soothing. The whole thing takes on a cohesive visual shape when painted with the priming layer of white paint or gesso, and the fragmenting effect of the newspaper print is obscured. Finally, with the decorating of the surface, the whole piece comes to life.

The interpretation of these basic techniques reflects the character and interests of the artist, as can be seen in the work of the three artists featured in this book.

Julie Arkell trained as a fashion textile designer and worked as an illustrator for several years before she discovered the tremendous liberation of expressing her imaginative and whimsical imagery on sculptural surfaces. Her initial inspiration for working with papier mâché came to her on seeing the ancient Grecian urns in the British Museum and wanting to find a simple way of interpreting them in three dimensions. Then her love of fashion accessories led her to develop a range of colourful and dramatic jewellery in which she explores sculptural shapes and her delight in colour and decoration on a small scale. She enjoys recreating the objects and images that appeal to her in her own personal way in three-dimensional still lifes. She lets the nature of the material dictate, allowing the creases of the paper to create the texture of the surface, and is now making increasing use of the application of found objects, recycling broken fragments of materials such as pottery and glass and transforming them to give them a new context.

Marion Elliot trained as a fine artist and then turned to ceramics, producing hand-built earthenware vases, bowls and sculptural pieces. Becoming increasingly frustrated with the limitations of clay as a medium, and the range of colours that she could obtain, she tried various techniques to try to achieve a more direct, colourful and vibrant effect. Eventually she tried papier mâché, feeling that the fundamental processes were similar to those used in pottery but knowing that she would have greater freedom with colour, shape and size. She also discovered that the flexibility and versatility of the medium were more appropriate to the way she works and the type of imagery that she uses. While the influence on the shapes of her bowls and vases is strongly derived from ancient and classical ceramic forms, her painted designs are inspired by other sources such as tattoos, packaging and naïve art. She enjoys incorporating enigmatic phrases and words from poems and proverbs to reflect the subject of her images.

Deborah Schneebeli-Morrell trained as a fine artist and also worked in clay, but felt that it did not offer the freedom she wanted. She then began to develop her ideas using papier mâché and found that she responded to the freshness and flexibility of the medium. Uninhibited by the lack of historical technical precedent, she enjoyed the idea of recycling discarded materials and turning them into precious objects. Her inspiration is eclectic, her imagery frequently based on universal themes which find reference in her own life

and are expressed in her shrine-like icons with their symbolic figures. The art of Mexico with its strong tradition of papier mâché artefacts has had a particularly strong influence on her. She recreates traditional Mexican peasant dolls, interpreting them with more sophisticated techniques and delighting in emphasizing the lightness of the material by using fresh and bright colours with a particular concern to use non-toxic materials. She creates the forms for her figures by sculpting moulds with modelling material and achieves a highly smooth finish to the work by using tiny pieces of paper and several layers of gesso.

All three artists share a delight in the simplicity and flexibility of the material, the potential creativity of the forms, experimentation with techniques to achieve the results they want, exploration of their diverse sources of inspiration, a love of bright colour, and the alchemy

of transforming ordinary materials into beautiful objects. They share a joyous approach to their work.

The projects in this book are demonstrated with detailed step-by-step instructions, allowing you to recreate the pieces. However, much of the excitement of working with papier mâché is in making your own discoveries and expressing your own ideas, so once you have discovered how the materials behave, experiment with your own ideas and invent your own shapes and techniques. The examples of other work by the artists illustrated in the Gallery section will inspire you to try other possibilities.

. . . .

Julie Arkell's jewellery designs reflect
her love of sculptural shapes and use of
unusual decorative devices.

MATERIALS AND EQUIPMENT

THE MATERIALS required for creating papier mâché objects are inexpensive and readily available. This list illustrates the basic ingredients; other, more specialized requirements are given in the materials lists for the projects.

It is a good idea to cover your work surface with a sheet of plastic, not only to protect it, but also to prevent objects from sticking to the surface. If you are a messy worker, wear an apron.

NEWSPAPER

Collect a supply of old newspapers. Broadsheet newspapers are better quality than tabloids and will mould around shapes more smoothly. Newspaper strips should always be torn not cut.

WALLPAPER PASTE

Cellulose cold water paste is used to paste the layers of paper pieces together. Most proprietary brands contain fungicide, and are therefore unsuitable for use by children. Non-toxic paste powder is available from educational suppliers, craft shops and some specialist decorating outlets. Mix up according to the instructions on the packet. For additional strength you can add a little PVA adhesive, and some brands now include it in the mix. Cover the paste bowl when not in use with an air-tight lid or damp cloth. Wrap up unwanted paste in newspaper and throw it away – do not wash it down the drain.

A rather messy alternative, which has a short life, is a flour and water paste, but this is best avoided unless it is your only option.

PASTE BOWL

This should be large enough to hold a reasonable quantity of paste for the project you are working on. A domestic kitchen bowl is ideal. Wash it thoroughly after use to get rid of all traces of paste and any PVA glue that may have been used.

PAPER PULP

The easiest pulp to use is sold as dried, prepared, ground paper and it is usually available from toy and hobby shops. Make up with water according to the instructions on the packet; to give extra adhesion add some ready-mixed decorators' filler.

You can also make your own paper pulp from newspaper, but this is a messy business which has little advantage, except cost and availability, over the ready-prepared variety.

MOULDS AND FRAMEWORKS

The basic shapes for a papier mâché design can usually be created from a wide range of household objects and materials: for instance, a mixing bowl, a ramekin dish, a blown-up balloon, smooth-sided corrugated card, toilet roll tubes and modelling plastic. Artists' mounting board is also useful. Make a collection of anything you think may be appropriate. Many moulds can be re-used if the dried papier mâché is removed carefully.

PETROLEUM JELLY

This is used as a release agent on a mould from which you want to remove the paper shape once it is dry. Liquid detergent can be used as an alternative.

PVA WOOD GLUE

Polyvinyl acetate woodworking glue (or white glue) is used to glue paper pieces and cardboard together.

When diluted with water, this adhesive can also be used as a sealant for porous surfaces.

EPOXY RESIN

This is used for really strong adhesion. Mix and apply according to the manufacturer's instructions. The quick-drying type takes about 10 minutes to harden and is very convenient to use; the standard version dries within about 10 hours. Both should be used with care as they can irritate sensitive skin. Not to be used by children.

PENCIL, FELT PEN

Use these to mark the cutting outlines for pattern pieces on card. Pencils are best for sketching decorative designs onto a white sealant primer before painting.

KNIFE AND/OR SCISSORS

These are used to trim edges and cut pieces of card and need to be sharp. Depending on the intricacy of the work, use a craft knife, a utility knife with snap-off blades, or a scalpel. Protect blades when stored.

METAL STRAIGHT EDGE

Use to mark out straight lines on card pieces, and as a cutting edge for clean straight finishes.

BLUNT FLAT-TIPPED KNIFE

This is used as a lever to prize away the sides of papier mâché objects from a mould after they have hardened.

CAKE RACK

This makes a handy drying rack for small pieces, allowing air to circulate all around them.

WHITE MATT EMULSION PAINT OR READY-PREPARED ACRYLIC GESSO

These are used as a primer on the finished papier mâché shape before the decoration is added, providing a bright white surface to work on. Household emulsion (from any decorators' suppliers) is very economical. Ready-prepared acrylic gesso (from artists' suppliers) is more expensive; it gives a thicker layer and a soft chalky surface.

PAINTS AND INK

Gouache and acrylic paints are favoured by the artists in this book. These are water-based paints, available in a wide range of colours.

Gouache (or designers' gouache), an opaque watercolour paint, is easily handled as long as each layer is allowed to dry before applying the next.

Acrylic paints are sold in jars and tubes and can be mixed with water, but using an acrylic medium will keep the colours stronger. They are very quick-drying. – make sure that you do not allow the paint to dry on the brushes, or you will not be able to wash it off.

Black waterproof Indian ink is used to create strong outline detail on several of the projects in this book.

WATER POT AND PALETTE

Any jam jar or pot will do as a water jar. Your palette should ideally have small wells or compartments to keep colours separate, but you could use a plate or saucer just as well.

VARNISH

A polyurethane clear wood varnish, either matt or gloss (available from any decorators' suppliers), will give a durable and waterproof finish to your work and will intensify the colours. Some brands tend to yellow a little with age.

Artists' acrylic varnish, also called picture varnish (matt or gloss), is more expensive than the household variety, but is less prone to yellowing.

BRUSHES

You will need at least three types of brushes for different uses:

- A small household painting brush to apply emulsion paint or a medium-sized nylon artists' brush for gesso. Wash the brushes in water after use.
- An artists' watercolour brush of hair or nylon (or a mix of the two) to apply the gouache or acrylic paint. Clean in water after use and store bristles uppermost in a jar. The better you look after it the longer it will last. It is useful to have a range of three or more, including a broad one for washes and a fine one for detail.
- A small household brush or a medium-sized artists' brush for varnish. Clean in white spirit as soon as you have finished working.

Paints: *water-based acrylic or gouache recommended for painting over primer base.*

Wallpaper paste: *ideally mixed in a wide, shallow bowl.*

Masking tape: *holds glued sections of corrugated card while drying.*

Indian ink: *must be waterproof to facilitate corrections.*

Newspaper: *always torn into strips, never cut.*

Modelling plastic: *invaluable for shaping and making moulds.*

Scissors, scalpel, Stanley knife: *must be sharp for cutting card.*

Emulsion paint *and* **acrylic gesso:** *to prime surfaces before decorating.*

Felt-tip pens, pencils, *and* **decorating and artists' brushes:** *for applying designs and colours.*

Polturethane varnish: *for matt or glossy finish.*

Epoxy resin: *for strong joins;* **PVA glue:** *for joining card and paper pieces.*

Ruler: *for measuring, but metal straight edge must be used for cutting.*

BASIC TECHNIQUES

WHEN YOU start on a project, make sure that you have everything you need, and, ideally, find a work surface where you can leave everything without having to clear up between the various stages of the work.

MIXING UP THE PASTE

Begin by mixing up the wallpaper paste. Use ½ litre (1 pint) of water and calculate the amount of powder required to make a thick mixture according to the instructions given. Pour the water into a bowl, sprinkle on the powder and stir well. Leave for 15 minutes, to allow the paste to swell stirring occasionally. Add a little PVA adhesive to strengthen it if you like.

If you want to make flour and water paste use the following recipe: mix together ½ litre (1 pint) of water and 85g (3oz) plain flour in a stainless steel saucepan. Allow to stand for an hour, stirring constantly bring to the boil, simmer for 10 minutes, leave to cool.

TEARING UP THE NEWSPAPER

Tear up a generous quantity of newspaper into strips, varying in size according to the shape you are making. You will find that it is much easier to tear in one direction than the other. This is caused by the direction of the grain of the paper, which is determined by the way the sheet passed through the machine during manufacture and the direction of the paper fibres. In most newspapers the grain runs from top to bottom. Tearing the paper gives a feathered edge and produces a smoother finish to the papier mâché than you would achieve by using pieces cut with scissors.

ASSEMBLY/PREPARING THE MOULD

If you are constructing a framework for your papier mâché shape, assemble it with glue and allow to dry.

PVA wood glue should be applied to both surfaces. Wipe off any excess glue, and hold the pieces fast with masking tape or weight down the surfaces as appropriate while the glue dries.

Epoxy resin should be applied to both surfaces, and the pieces held fast while it dries.

If you are using a mould from which you will remove the papier mâché shape, give it a generous coating of petroleum jelly before applying the first layers of pasted paper. This will prevent the paper from sticking to the shape. If you are making a mould from modelling plastic, it is not necessary to use petroleum jelly for small shapes as the material has a certain amount of grease in it. However, it is advisable to use it for more complicated shapes (such as the mask project) to avoid any possibility of sticking.

PASTING AND APPLYING THE NEWSPAPER

Use your hand to smear paste onto one or both sides of the paper strip, and squeeze off the excess with your fingers. You can allow the paste to soak in for a few minutes if you like, placing the pieces around the edge of the bowl before applying. This is advisable if you are using poor quality newspaper, to allow time for absorption of the paste.

Apply the paper pieces to the mould or framework, overlapping them and varying the direction of the pieces. Depending on the piece you are making, the effect you want to achieve and your preferred way of working, you might apply them in an orderly or random fashion.

The scale of the piece you are making will determine the size of the pieces you use, but you can also deliberately create different surfaces according to the size of the strips. For instance, when covering a curved shape you will achieve a smooth surface with very tiny pieces; by using large pieces and allowing pleats to form, you will create a more textured surface.

PASTING THE PAPER LAYERS

The total number of layers you apply will depend on both the size of the object and the strength required for the piece you are making. If you are covering a small card template (for a piece of jewellery, for instance) you will need to use only two layers of newspaper; for a bowl that is going to be used to carry fruit you should use at least eight layers.

It is helpful to use newspapers of two different colours so that you can keep track of the number of layers you have applied and so ensure an even cover. This is useful when working all the layers at the same time. Alternatively you can apply one layer at a time, allowing it to dry for 24 hours before applying the next.

When you have completed a layer, smooth over it with your fingers to remove any bubbles and excess glue.

DRYING TIME

The amount of time required to dry the pasted paper obviously varies according to the temperature of your room and the weather. The drying times recommended for the various stages of the projects in this book are based on working in a mild, temperate climate, so you will have to adjust the estimates depending on your own conditions. Using a warm airing cupboard will speed up the drying time.

If you dry the piece layer by layer, you will have a good idea of drying rates. If you apply all the layers in one session, test to see how dry the piece is after two or three days. If working on a mould, prize away the sides with a blunt knife and check to see if the paper comes away easily. If it does not, allow to dry for a further day. Once out of the mould, allow an extra day's drying time so that the side that has been in contact with the mould is completely dried out.

Drying should be done at an even temperature. This is important if you are using a balloon as a mould. Any dramatic changes in temperature, or extreme heat, may cause the balloon to burst or to shrivel up.

FINISHING THE SHAPE

If you are trimming the edges (for the mirror or bowl project, for instance), you should "bind" the cut edge with small strips of pasted paper and allow to dry.

When joining pieces (for the doll, for instance), stick them together with PVA wood glue and hold fast with masking tape while drying for about half an hour, making sure to wipe off any excess glue. When dry, remove the masking tape and cover the join with small strips of pasted paper.

You may like to smooth the surface of the papier mâché with sandpaper. Start with medium grade paper and then use a fine grade; brush off the dust particles.

PRIMING THE PAPIER MÂCHÉ

Apply white emulsion paint or ready-prepared acrylic gesso to prime the porous surface of the layers of pasted paper and to provide a surface for the final decoration. Use a household brush for emulsion paint and a soft artists' brush for gesso. Allow to dry between layers.

Apply one or two coats of emulsion. If the first coat cracks badly, be sure to apply a second coat. Up to four coats of gesso give a really smooth surface.

DRAWING THE DESIGN

Use a pencil or a fine blue crayon to draw the design lightly onto the white surface if required.

PAINTING

If you are using gouache, squeeze a small amount onto a palette and add a few drops of water. Do not thin it too much – you want to achieve an opaque layer of colour. Allow the first layer of colour to dry before applying subsequent layers.

Acrylic should preferably be mixed with acrylic medium. Work as with gouache, allowing the layers to dry.

VARNISHING

The paint must be absolutely dry before you apply the varnish. Test your brush first to check that it is not prone to shedding bristles or hairs, which will be difficult to remove. Apply an even coat over the whole piece, working in two stages if necessary so that you can stand the piece on a dry edge or surface when drying. Dry in a dust-free area.

If applying two coats, allow the first to dry out completely before applying the second.

Clean the brush in white spirit immediately after you have finished working.

GALLERY

THESE EXAMPLES of the work of Julie Arkell, Marion Elliot and Deborah Schneebeli-Morrell demonstrate a wide range of papier mâché objects. They reflect the artists' diverse use of materials and techniques, as well as their creative use of sculptural form, design and colour.

All of these objects are, of course, individual to the artists themselves, but they will also inspire you to make your own experiments whether you are seeking to create a purely decorative feature or a piece that is practical as well.

~

Fish-eye Vase and Shell Vase

MARION ELLIOT
Height: about 35cm (1ft 2in)

These flamboyant vases are inspired by the shape of ancient Greek and Roman vases, while the handles have a rather Baroque flavour, and natural designs – fish, shells and seaweed – are used for decoration. A mould was used for the body of the vase, and the handles are made from pieces of card. The raised decoration is made from small lumps of pulpy paper.

. . . .

Mirrors

JULIE ARKELL
Height: about 45cm (18in)
You Wore Your Red Hat and I Wore My Veil (left) is a three-dimensional realization of a painting done by the artist. The mosaic-like decoration on *Sun Fragments* (right) was achieved by applying a layer of tile putty to the piece and embedding it with "urban jewels" (fragments of discarded china, broken car headlamps and other sparkling objects) to give them new life. The flower vase is made from an anchovy jar.

. . . .

**Circus Dog and Blue
Canary, Royal Dog**
JULIE ARKELL
Height: about 23cm (9in)
Wishing for a dog of her
own, the artist created
these endearing beasts in
papier mâché. The body
is made from crumpled-
up dry newspaper taped
in place and moulded
with pasted paper strips;
the features and limbs
are added with card.

. . . .

The Hand of Vitality
(centre) and
Valentine Pieces
(right and left)
DEBORAH
SCHNEEBELI-
MORRELL
*Height: 44cm (1ft 5in) and
30cm (1ft)*
The hand is used here to
symbolize creativity and
vitality. It is also shown
as the hand of
friendship, love and
greeting in the *Valentine
Pieces* which have
references to the
imagery of folk art
traditions.

. . . .

Mirror

MARION ELLIOT
*Height: about 70cm
(2ft 4in)*
An old wooden mirror frame has been covered with papier mâché and brightly decorated to give it new life. The artist has used a line from a poem by Christopher Marlowe to illustrate Elizabethan courtly love in the design of this piece.

. . . .

Candlestick and Candelabra

JULIE ARKELL
*Height: about 49cm
(1ft 7in)*
The surreal mood of the book *One Hundred Years of Solitude* by Gabriel Garcia Marquez inspired the recreation of these candleholders with their everlastingly dripping candles, in a grandiose South American style. The basic structure is made from card and a mould, the entwining stems are fashioned from wire, with paper wound in spiral twists for the roses.

. . . .

A Valentine View

DEBORAH
SCHNEEBELI–
MORRELL

Height: 62cm (2ft)

This decorative piece
also has a functional use.
The figure, representing
the strength of woman,
stands above the white
horse, symbolizing
fertility. Both are made
from papier mâché cast
over a mould of
modelling material, the
base is made by card
construction, and the
mirror is modelled with
paper pulp and
decorated with gold leaf.

. . . .

Centaur Vase

MARION ELLIOT

Height: about 57cm (22in)

This vase depicts a
bacchanalian celebration
of spring. It reflects the
artist's preoccupation
with Greek art and
pottery, and is a modern
interpretation of classical
themes. The elaborate
shape, and the
detachable lid are
inspired by medieval
Moorish silverware
designs.

. . . .

Jewellery

JULIE ARKELL
Size: average 8cm (3in)
The theatricality of costume jewellery holds a fascination that is evident in these pieces. Working on this scale allows the development of small sculptural ideas and the playing around with colour, shape and decoration. This selection suggests some ideas for alternative designs to the jewellery project.

. . . .

Three Part Invention

DEBORAH SCHNEEBELI-MORRELL
Height: 52cm (1ft 8in)
The artist was listening to Bach's *Three Part Inventions* while working on this, and, interested by the coincidence of working on a piece with three parts, decided to name it after the music. The bird held aloft represents the flight of the spirit.

. . . .

Sun God

DEBORAH
SCHNEEBELI-
MORRELL

*Height: about 65cm
(2ft 2in)*

This symbol of the life
force also refers to the
myth of Apollo, the
Greek sun god, and a
water nymph who
metamorphosed into a
sunflower and turned
her head to follow the
path of his travels
through the sky. The
figure is cast over a
mould and the flower,
urns and flames, and the
frame are constructed
from corrugated card
and paper pulp.

. . . .

**Winged Heart Box,
Golden Apples Krater,
Love's Offering Bowl**

MARION ELLIOT

*Height: Box and Bowl
20cm (8in); Krater 25cm
(10in)*

The winged heart on the
box draws direct
inspiration from tattoo
designs, while the shape
of the box has a shrine-
like quality to it. The
vase takes its shape from
the ancient Greek krater
shape. Both the vase and
the bowl are decorated
with two of the artist's
favourite motifs – cupids
and suns.

. . . .

An Honest Englishman

MARION ELLIOT

Height: about 36cm (14in)

Affection for English eccentricity and tradition inspired the imagery for this vase, which depicts an amiable English gentleman being honoured with a wreath of laurels by a respectful cherub.

. . . .

Ship and Sun

JULIE ARKELL

Height: about 51cm (1ft 8in)

A piece of sea-worn driftwood provided the starting point for this piece, which has been built up into a delightful nautical still life decorated with bits and pieces found on the beach and from other sources – string, sweet wrappers, bottle tops and fragments of sea urchin.

. . . .

**Integrated Woman
with Flower Urns**

DEBORAH
SCHNEEBELI-
MORRELL

Height: about 60cm (2ft)

This icon in the form of
a triptych is a celebration
of the understanding
that has come to
woman. In her hands she
confidently holds a fish,
symbol of the masculine
aspect of the female
unconscious. The
element of growth is
portrayed in the flower-
filled urns. The piece is
made from cast and
constructed papier
mâché, and the frame is
decorated with silver
leaf.

. . . .

Painted Ladies

JULIE ARKELL

*Height: about 51cm
(1ft 8in)*

This bold triumvirate of
ladies is a light-hearted
comment on the
strength of woman. The
different poses and
fashions may give you
some ideas for designing
your own variations on
the project described
later.

. . . .

FLOWER IN A POT

JULIE ARKELL

THIS BRIGHT, whimsical tulip plant provides an ever-lasting touch of spring to brighten up a room and makes a delightful gift. You can vary the colour of the pot and the petals, and the design of the flowers, but you should keep the shapes simple and avoid pieces that are too small or thin until you know how precisely you can work. You could also try a more ambitious piece by using a large bowl and "planting" it with a number of different flowers.

A single tulip, with its bold flower and broad leaves is an ideal flower to start with. The construction is very simple: it is built up on a framework of smooth-sided corrugated card for the leaves and flower, a thin length of wooden dowel for the stem, and a plastic pot for the flower pot.

Height: 43cm (1ft 5in)

~

TECHNIQUES

Glue the framework pieces together with quick-drying epoxy resin.

Take care to preserve the sharp outlines of the foliage and flower by wrapping the paper pieces neatly around the shapes. Push the paper into the sharper corners with the edge of a piece of thin card if necessary.

This piece requires two layers of paper. Allow the first to dry for 24 hours before applying the second.

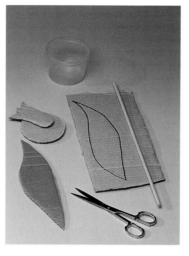

1 Gather together the base materials for the piece first – a pot the size you require, the wood for the stem, and card for the flower and earth. Cut out the shapes for the flower and leaves with scissors. Here, the leaves are 26cm (10in) long and the flower 11cm (4½in) long. Draw around the base of the pot for the circumference of the earth shape, and cut out.

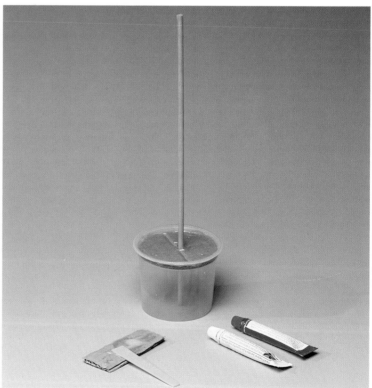

2 Assemble the pot and the stem. With the point of the scissors or a knife, pierce a hole in the middle of the earth piece. Glue around the circumference and fit it into the pot just below the lip. Glue the bottom end of the dowel and push it through the hole in the earth until it sticks to the base of the pot. Glue around the join of the dowel and the earth to secure them.

3 The flower and leaves can now
be positioned. Push the top of
the dowel through the base of the
flower for about 5cm (2in) and glue
in place. Hold the leaves in place
and glue them to the stem and to
the earth base. Secure all the pieces
with strips of masking tape until the
glue has set.

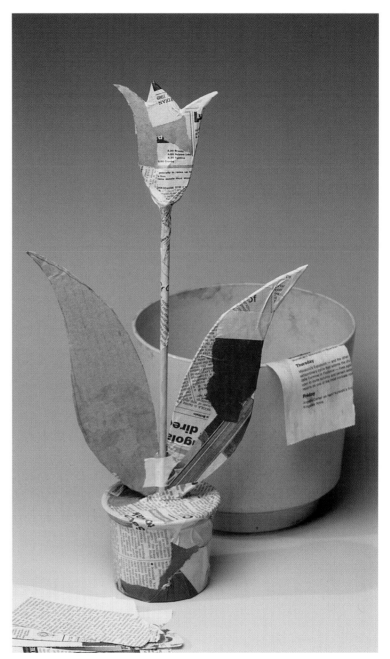

4 You can now start to paper the
piece. Wind the strips around the
stem; apply overlapping pieces over
the rest of the plant and pot. Tear
the paper into smaller pieces for the
flower and the ends of the leaves as
necessary. When you have
completed one layer, leave to dry.
Apply a second layer.

5 When dry, apply a coat of white emulsion paint. Allow to dry.

6 Mix up your preferred colours of gouache paints and apply broad areas of base colour. Here, the leaves are painted in two tones of green, and pink is washed over the petals, leaving some streaks of white emulsion showing through.

When the base colours have dried, you can apply the detailed decoration, such as the darker red tones of the petals, the veins on the leaves and the stripes on the pot.

7 When the paint has dried, give the whole piece a coat of varnish.

JEWELLERY

JULIE ARKELL

Dramatically large pieces of jewellery can be made from papier mâché because of the lightweight nature of the material. These striking earrings, brooch and bangle are richly decorated with colourful glass gems in a metallic setting to imitate precious jewellery settings.

The earrings and the brooch are made by the same method, built up on card templates; the bangle is made by twisting together some long strips of newspaper and covering them with pieces of paper (you can vary the bulk of the bangle by twisting the paper more tightly).

The heart is a favourite motif, but you may like to choose your own design – a star, sun or flowers, for instance. Decorate all the pieces in the same way so that you create a matching set of jewellery.

You can buy the findings (the hooks and loops, the ear clips and pin fastening) and the glass gems at a hobby shop.

Earrings 9cm (3¹/₂in) long; Brooch 9cm (3¹/₂in) long;
Bangle 13cm (5in) in diameter

~

MATERIALS

• *1 piece of mounting board
15 × 15cm (6 × 6in)* • *2
pairs of hooks and eyes* • *2
clips for earrings* • *pin
fastener for brooch (jewellery
findings are available from
hobby shops)* • *scissors*
• *newspaper: for earrings
and brooch, torn into pieces
about 5cm (2in) square; for
bangle, 6 strips 15cm (6in)
wide by the length of a broadsheet newspaper, and several
pieces 8 × 20cm (3 × 8in)*
• *masking tape (for the
bangle) cut into 13cm (5in)
strips* • *bowl for paste*
• *mixed quantity of
wallpaper paste* • *quick-
drying epoxy resin* • *white
emulsion paint* • *glass gems
(available from hobby shops)*
• *metal foil from sweet
wrappings* • *stick glue or
spray glue* • *gouache paint:
spectrum red, marigold yellow
and gold are used here*
• *jewellers' pliers (optional)*
• *polyurethane gloss varnish*
• *brushes: household brushes
for emulsion paint and
varnish; artists' brushes for
paint* • *white spirit to clean
varnish brush*

. . . . . .

TECHNIQUES

*Glue the findings to the cardboard with
quick-drying epoxy resin.*

*Apply two layers of paper to the
earrings and brooch and three to the
bangle, allowing each to dry. Use a
wire cake rack, if you have one, to
dry small objects such as these – this
will allow air to circulate freely
around them.*

*Stick on the gems with quick-drying
epoxy resin. Use stick glue or spray
glue for the metal foil. If using spray
glue, spray several strips at a time and
leave for a few minutes before
applying.*

1 **Earrings and Brooch** Cut out
the shapes for the earrings – two
circles 2.5cm (1in) in diameter, two
heart shapes about 5cm (2in) wide
and 6cm (2½in) long. Glue a hook
to the circle, and a loop to the top of
the heart. Cut a heart shape for the
brooch 8cm (3in) wide and 9cm
(3½in) long.

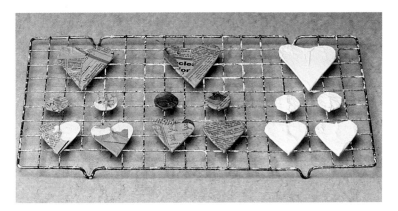

2 Paste one layer of newspaper to
both sides of the pieces, piercing
the findings through the paper.
Wrap the paper around the shape
and coax it into the corner of the
heart with your fingers or a piece of
card. Allow to dry. Apply a second
layer of paper.

Allow to dry and then apply a
coat of white emulsion paint.

3 Stick the gems on and then paint the background colour onto the back and front. Allow to dry.

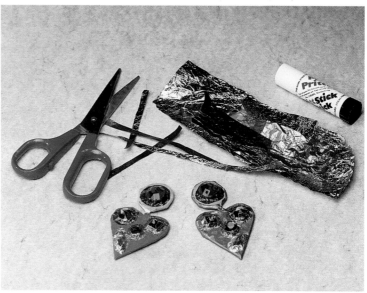

4 Cut the metal foil into thin strips, cover the backs with glue, then apply the foil around the jewels. Mould it into the gems with your fingers, pleat it around the curves and cut at the corners. Neaten the edges with a sharp knife if necessary.

Paint the gold borders and decoration.

5 With the point of a knife or a pin, clean out any paint from the findings. Join the two pieces together, closing the hook with a small pair of scissors, or jewellers' pliers (if you have them). Add a dot of glue at the closing to secure fully.

Glue the clasps onto the back of the earrings and the pin to the brooch and then give them a coat of varnish.

The newspaper can be folded along its length several times and must be tightly twisted before being bent into a circle the right size to fit your wrist.

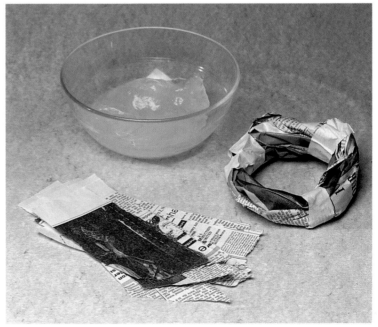

1 **Bangle** Hold the long pieces of newspaper at either end and twist tightly together at least three times, then wind it into a circle. Try it on your wrist to judge for size. Remove from your wrist, then, holding it together, secure in position with masking tape.

Cover over the shape with pasted newspaper pieces. Apply a total of three layers, allowing each to dry.

2 The method for the decoration of the bangle is the same as for the earrings and brooch. Apply a coat of white emulsion paint and allow to dry. Stick on the jewels, paint the background, stick on the metal foil, paint the gold decoration, and finally apply varnish.

3 By decorating the pieces with complementary 'jewels' and colours, you create a matching set.

VASE

JULIE ARKELL

THE BASIC shape of this vase was built up on a round balloon and the organic form of the lip was achieved by cutting the opening and moulding it with paper strips. The shape and its elaborate and colourful painting make this vase a beautiful decorative object. The curious characters and whimsical design motifs which sprang from the artist's imagination may be difficult for you to achieve, so you might like to devise your own decoration. If you paint it quite plainly you could use the vase to hold some dried flowers, which might otherwise detract from the decoration. Papier mâché will not hold water so is not suitable for fresh flowers.

Fairly large pieces of paper were used to cover the balloon, resulting in an interesting textured surface that accentuates the nature of the material.

Height: 28cm (11in)

~

MATERIALS

• round balloon • cotton thread or string to tie the balloon • bowl for paste • mixed quantity of wallpaper paste • newspaper torn into pieces about 8 × 13cm (3 × 5in) • scissors • white emulsion paint • pencil • gouache paints: various colours and gold • water pot and palette • polyurethane gloss varnish • brushes: household brushes for emulsion and varnish; artists' brushes for gouache • white spirit to clean varnish brush

. . . . . .

TECHNIQUES

Blow up the the balloon, tie it with thread, and then rest it on a large saucepan or bowl to hold it still while working at a table.

Allow each layer of paper to dry for about 24 hours before applying the next. Avoid extreme heat and excessive temperature changes when drying the paper or the balloon might burst or shrink and shrivel up. Apply three layers of papier mâché to the base and to the lip with drying time between each layer.

Judge the cutting line by eye, or, if you prefer, sit the balloon in a small bowl and draw around the rim to mark the line. You can use the discarded piece to make the hat for the Painted Lady project.

Make sure that your hand will fit inside the vase so that you can paint the inside of the vase with emulsion paint.

1 Blow up a balloon and apply the pasted newspaper pieces, overlapping them generously and smoothing down the creases. Apply seven layers, allowing each to dry with the balloon suspended by a thread from the neck.

2 To make a flat base for the vase, cut off a small disc-shaped piece from the papier mâché globe with a pair of scissors. Remove the balloon. Trim the edge until the paper shape stands squarely.

Cover the base hole with three layers of pasted newspaper strips. Apply a neatening band of paper pieces around the base of the vase to cover the ends of these strips.

3 To create the opening for the vase, make a series of diagonal cuts about 8cm (3in) long from the small hole at the top with a pair of scissors. Gently press out the cut pieces with your hand.

4 Make the lip by covering the cut area with three layers of pasted paper, moulding the shape and filling in the breaks between the pieces. Work from the inside to the outside. Apply a neatening band of paper pieces to cover the ends of these layers on the inside and outside of the vase.

5 When dry, give the vase one coat of white emulsion paint, both inside and out.

6 Draw on the decoration with a pencil and start to paint, allowing drying time between the layers for paint to dry.

7 Apply a coat of gloss varnish to finish the vase.

MOBILE

JULIE ARKELL

THIS COLOURFUL mobile, with its rainbow of thin ribbons, is not only delightful to look at, but when hung in a place that catches a slight draught, will produce a soft, soothing, clicking sound.

Here a variety of motifs have been chosen: dog, sun, fish, clown and a heart, but you could choose just one design – a fish, for instance – and decorate the pieces differently to give variety of colour.

The pieces are light enough to hang from a wooden framework that is simply stuck together with glue. When inserting the screw eyes into the cardboard templates, make sure that you find the balancing point of each piece, unless you intend them to hang at angles.

Length: 28cm (11in) from framework to base

MATERIALS

- *corrugated card, a piece about 38cm (15in) square*
- *felt-tip pen or pencil*
- *scissors* • *11 screw eyes*
- *quick-drying epoxy resin*
- *2 pieces 2cm (½in) softwood, each piece about 15cm (6in) long* • *small hacksaw to cut wood, if necessary* • *newspaper torn into pieces about 5 × 8cm (2 × 3in) long* • *bowl for paste* • *mixed quantity of wallpaper paste* • *wire rack*
- *white emulsion paint*
- *gouache paint in various colours* • *polyurethane varnish* • *brushes: household brushes for emulsion and varnish; artists' brushes for gouache* • *5 pieces of thin ribbon in various colours, each about 30cm (1ft) long*

. . . . . .

TECHNIQUES

Use quick-drying epoxy resin to glue the wooden hanger together, and to glue the screw eyes to the mobile shapes.

Apply the paste with your hand to one side of the paper. Apply two layers of paper pieces to the framework and the mobile shapes, allowing about 24 hours' drying time between the layers. Dry on a wire rack to allow air to pass around the pieces.

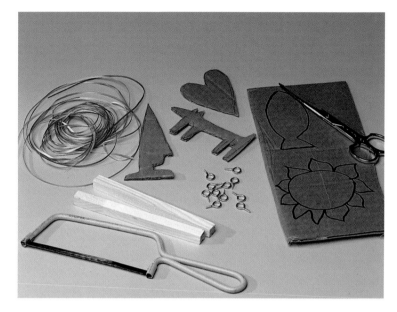

1 Assemble the materials. Have the wood cut to the required lengths, or cut it yourself with a hacksaw. Cut out the card shapes with scissors. The pieces are all about 10–13cm (4–5in) long.

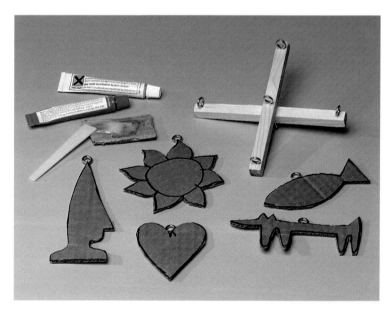

2 Glue the two pieces of wood together to form a cross. Push the shank of five screw eyes into the corrugations of the mobile shapes and glue in place. Screw five screw eyes into the ends and middle of one side of the wooden framework and one eye into the middle on the other side.

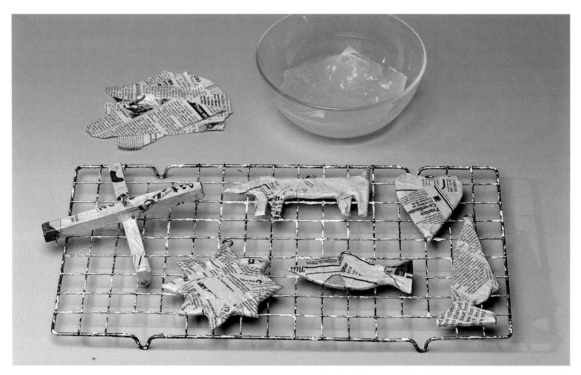

3 Cover the framework and the shapes with two layers of pasted newspaper pieces, keeping the eyes clear, and dry them on a wire rack.

4 Give the framework and the shapes a coat of white emulsion paint and allow to dry.

5 Decorate the pieces with gouache paint, leaving the first coat to dry before applying subsequent layers.

6 When dry, give all the pieces a coat of gloss varnish and allow to dry. Then assemble the mobile, tying the ribbon with double knots. Cut the ribbons to the required lengths, making the central piece hang higher than the rest.

7 All that remains is to hang your mobile in a place where it catches a slight draught.

PAINTED LADY

J U L I E   A R K E L L

This statuesque painted lady is built up on a long balloon which has been twisted to create the "waist" of the figure. Once the basic shape of the body has been made, you can add the other features. The head is made from a base of rolled-up newspaper, and the arms are simply moulded on to a length of wire threaded through the body. The hat is made from a disc cut from the base of a papered round balloon, but if you make the Vase project, you can make use of the discarded piece here.

For ideas on possible variations in the design, look at the photograph of other painted ladies in the Gallery section. You can create your own fashions, both in colour and in style, but keep the design bold for the best effect.

Height: 53cm (1ft 9in)

~

MATERIALS

- 1 long balloon, 1 round balloon • cotton thread • bowl for paste • mixed quantity of wallpaper paste • newspaper torn into strips about 5 × 13cm (2 × 5in). For the roses on the hat tear into strips about 5 × 20cm (2 × 8in) • scissors • galvanised steel wire, 35cm (1ft 2in) long • pliers to cut the wire • masking tape • toilet roll cut into a strip 1 × 6cm (½ × 2½in) long • quick-drying epoxy resin • pen or pencil • white emulsion paint • gouache paints: blue, spectrum red, spectrum yellow, zinc white • varnish • brushes: household brushes for emulsion and varnish; artists' brushes for gouache • white spirit for cleaning varnish brush

. . . . . .

TECHNIQUES

Blow up the balloons and tie with a thread, and then rest on a flat surface. Apply the paste onto one side of the paper with your hand.

Hang the balloons in a doorway and allow 24 hours' drying time between each layer of paper. Avoid excessive heat and extremes of temperature while drying out the balloons or they may burst or shrivel up.

Cover the balloons with five layers of paper, the flat base with three layers; apply three more layers to the whole piece after assembling the head and arms and a final layer once the hat is on.

The neck is made from card. A piece cut from a toilet roll tube will give a good curve. Glue the neck together and then to the body with quick-drying epoxy resin.

Glue the flowers to the hat and the hat to the head also with quick-drying epoxy resin.

This piece requires two coats of emulsion paint. Allow the first to dry before applying the second.

1 Blow up a long balloon for the body; twist and tie it for the waist. Blow up a round balloon on which to model the hat.

Apply five layers of pasted newspaper pieces to the long balloon, starting at the waist with the first layer. Apply five layers of paper to the base of the round balloon. Allow to dry between layers.

2 Cut off the rounded piece from the bottom of the long balloon to provide a flat base for the lady to stand on, piercing the paper with scissors. Remove the balloon and trim the base level.

Cover the base hole with three layers of pasted newspaper strips, smoothing them tightly over the hole. When dry, apply a band of paper strips around the ends of these pieces to neaten.

3 Pierce two holes for the arms on either side of the body, about 4cm (1½in) from the top, using the point of a pair of scissors. Thread wire through the body, smooth into a curve and bind the ends together at the waist level with masking tape.

To make the neck, glue the ends of the cardboard circle together to form a ring about 2cm (¾in) in diameter. Glue on to the top of the balloon.

For the head, roll up a crumpled piece of pasted newspaper to about the size of a golf ball. Place this on top of the neck. Make the breasts from smaller rolled-up pieces of newspaper, and paste in position.

4 Apply a layer of pasted newspaper pieces to the whole piece, winding them around the wire arms. Allow to dry and then apply two more layers, with drying time between them.

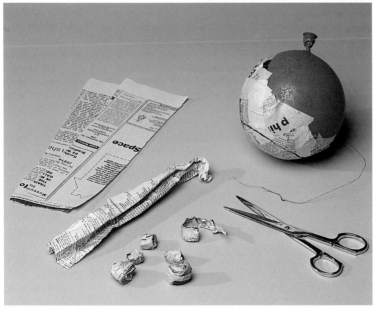

5 Mark the shape of the hat on the round balloon and cut out with scissors. This one is 11cm (4½in) in diameter.

Make spirals for the roses. Paste a strip of paper and crumple it up in your hand, then curl it into a series of spirals. Leave to dry.

6 When the spirals are dry, cut them in half (each will make two roses), and glue the flat side to the hat.

8 After the paper has dried, apply two coats of white emulsion paint allowing the first to dry before applying the second.

7 Glue the hat to the head with quick-drying epoxy resin and allow to dry.

Apply a final layer of newspaper pieces to the whole body, including the hat, but not the roses.

9 Paint the red and blue parts of the clothes. Paint the hat and the flowers, and also the features of the face, and allow to dry.

10 Add the yellow stripes and the dots on the jacket, and allow to dry before varnishing.

FOOTED BOWL

MARION ELLIOT

THIS DECORATIVE bowl is substantial enough to be used to hold fruit. Its shape is classic and symmetrical. Natural designs, which lend themselves well to round forms, have been used for the decoration. The wider rim at the edge of the base gives the bowl balance, both in visual and physical terms.

The lip of the bowl and the rim of the foot and the join between the two pieces are built up with the addition of rolls of pulpy paper that give the piece a more substantial appearance and imitates ceramic forms.

The colours can be varied to suit your own taste and you may like to consider other design motifs. The heavy black outlining is influenced by the artist's interest in early English woodcuts and is achieved by the use of black waterproof Indian ink.

Height: 14cm (5½in); Diameter 22cm (8½in)

~

MATERIALS

● 1 mould for bowl. Here a mixing bowl: diameter 22cm (8½in); height 9cm (3½in)
● 1 small mould for foot. Here a ramekin: diameter 10cm (4in); height 5cm (2in). The base should be wider than the rim
● petroleum jelly ● bowl for paste ● mixed quantity of wallpaper paste ● newspaper torn up into strips about 2.5cm (1in) wide, and as long as one side of the bowl to be covered plus 2.5cm (1in) for the overlap. (For the rolls, see Techniques.) ● blunt knife
● scissors ● sandpaper (medium and fine grade)
● PVA wood glue ● emulsion paint ● pencil ● gouache paints: turquoise, spectrum red, cadmium yellow, and zinc white are used here
● water pot and paint palette
● black waterproof indian ink
● polyurethane gloss varnish
● brushes: household painting brushes for emulsion and varnish; artists' brushes for gouache and Indian ink
● white spirit to clean varnish brush

· · · · · ·

TECHNIQUES

Paste the paper strips in a radiating pattern around the bowl, starting at the centre. Apply eight layers in one session. Use newspapers of two different colours, if possible, to help you to keep track of the number of layers applied.

Allow to dry for at least two days. With a blunt knife, prize the paper away from the bowl; if it comes away easily, remove from the mould and allow the paper to dry again for a day, otherwise, leave it for another day before trying again.

Allow one day to dry after working the rolls for the lip and rim, and also after joining the pieces.

To make a paper roll, wipe paste on both sides of a strip of newspaper, about 2.5 × 26cm (1 × 10in), fold it in half twice and crumple it up, rolling it in your palms. The rolls are fastened in position with pasted strips of newspaper about 1cm (½in) wide, torn to the required lengths.

When joining the bowl and the foot together with PVA wood glue, allow to dry for about two hours.

Using waterproof ink allows you to make corrections to the outlining details without the danger of muddying the colours, which might occur if you use black gouache. To make a correction, allow the ink to dry and then cover the area with white gouache, or process white. You can then reapply any base colour where necessary, and go over the outline again in black.

1 Cover the insides of both moulds and well over the rims with petroleum jelly. Apply eight layers of paper strips in one session to both bowls, allowing an overlap of about 2.5cm (1in) at the rim.

When complete, tear some paper into smaller pieces to make a final reinforcing band around the inside rims of both bowls to neaten the ends of the strips. Firm the paper down around the rims and make sure that the overlapping edges of paper protrude from the bowl.

2 After removing from the moulds, trim the edges with scissors and then neaten the cut edges with small strips of pasted paper.

Work lightly on the surfaces of both bowls with sandpaper to get them nice and smooth. Use medium grade sandpaper first, and then finish with fine grade.

3 Make a lip for the bowl and a rim for the foot by building them up with small rolls of newspaper.

Tuck two of the rolls under the trimmed edge of the bowl and hold them in position with one hand while you stick the end of a long paper strip on the outside of the lip and over the roll, then tear it off so that it is pasted to the inside of the bowl. Continue working around the rim and then apply a second layer of small strips over the lip. Work the foot rim in the same way.

Neaten the joining strips with a band of small strips pasted parallel to the rim on the inside and outside of the bowls. Allow to dry for one day.

4 Join the pieces together with glue and allow to dry.

To give a smooth contour to the join, apply paper rolls as before, pushing the first well into the join, and allowing a slight ridge to form with the second. Cover them with small strips of paper as before, but using three layers. Leave the bowl to dry for two days.

5 Remove any remaining petroleum jelly with cotton wool and white spirit if necessary, then apply two coats of white emulsion paint, allowing drying time between the coats. When dry, draw the design for your decoration on the bowl with a pencil.

6 Apply the colour in layers, starting with the lightest and working up to the darkest.

Mix up the yellow, blue and red paints with some white to achieve light tints and paint the areas required.

7 Allow the first application of paint to dry for at least an hour before adding the darker areas of yellow, blue and red. Allow to dry.

When quite dry, add the outline detail decoration with black waterproof Indian ink and a thin brush. Allow to dry.

Apply three coats of gloss varnish, allowing each coat to dry before applying the next.

MIRROR

MARION ELLIOT

A TRAY WAS used as the mould for the frame of this mirror, which has been decorated with a pattern to suggest the rays of the sun. The gems that are applied to the rim are created on modelling-plastic shapes.

You could also use a square or rectangular frame and have a mirror cut to reflect the shape of the frame, but it is advisable to keep the size of the mirror fairly small to avoid problems of weight when glueing and hanging. Wait until you have made the ridge for the mirror before you measure up and have the glass cut so that you ensure a good fit. Ask the glass cutters to have the edges polished for a better finish and to avoid cutting yourself.

The gold foil provides a good transition from the mirror to the frame. Using the foil from old sweet wrappers is an effective and economical alternative to using gold leaf, although of course there is nothing to stop you from using more traditional materials.

Diameter: 33cm (13in)

MATERIALS

● *1 tray for mould Here
diameter 33cm (13in), with
2.5cm (1in) rim* ● *petroleum
jelly* ● *modelling plastic to
model gems* ● *bowl for paste*
● *mixed quantity of
wallpaper paste* ● *newspaper
torn into 2.5cm (1in) wide
strips, long enough to cover
the tray including overlap on
both sides* ● *scissors* ● *craft
knife* ● *PVA wood glue*
● *masking tape* ● *white
emulsion paint* ● *pencil*
● *gouache paint: spectrum
red, spectrum yellow, emerald
green, turquoise, violet, and
zinc white are used here*
● *black waterproof Indian ink*
● *gold foil from sweet
wrappers to cover rim 17cm
(6¾in) diameter, cut into
10cm (4in) curved strips*
● *spoon* ● *spray adhesive*
● *polyurethane gloss varnish*
● *mirror glass cut to size.
Here 17cm (6¾in) in
diameter with polished edges*
● *metal mirror hanger or
"D"-ring hanger* ● *quick-
drying epoxy resin*
. . . . . .

TECHNIQUES

*Wipe paste on both sides of the paper
strips and apply the strips to the top of
the tray mould, working from the
centre out to the sides, overlapping the
pieces slightly and leaving a 2.5cm
(1in) overlap on both sides (which is
later trimmed off). Work the second
layer at right angles to the first, and
continue with alternating layers until
you have covered the tray with eight
layers. Allow to dry for two days.*

*Use PVA wood glue to stick the
gems to the frame, and hold them fast
with masking tape while it dries.*

*Smooth out the foil carefully using
the back of a spoon. Once you have cut
and moulded it into shape, use spray
glue to stick it to the frame. Spray the
back of the foil and leave for a couple of
minutes before applying.*

*Use quick-drying epoxy resin for
glueing the mirror and the hanger and
weight them down with heavy objects
while drying.*

1 Smear petroleum jelly over the
top of the tray and well over
both sides of the rim. Apply eight
layers of pasted newspaper strips in
one session to the top of the tray at
alternating angles and a final band
just inside the rim. Allow to dry for
two days.

Prize the paper off with a blunt
knife, and allow to dry flat for a
further day.

Trim to within 1cm (¼in) of the
edge and bind the cut edge with one
layer of small strips of pasted
newspaper.

2 The "gems" should be made at
  the same time as you cover the
tray with paper. Shape five balls of
modelling plastic into ovoid shapes
and coat with petroleum jelly.
Cover each of them with five layers
of small pasted paper pieces and
allow to dry for two days.

   Cut equally in halves through the
paper and the moulds with a knife
and remove the mould. Each half
makes a gem.

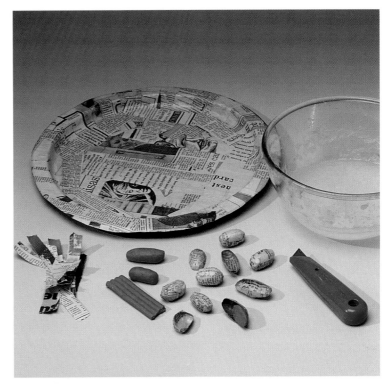

3 Draw a circle with a pair of
  compasses to mark the position
of the ridge into which the mirror
will fit. Make some pulpy paper
rolls (as described for the Footed
bowl) and paste a ridge of them
around the circle, moulding them
into a point at the centre with your
fingers. Cover with two layers of
small strips of pasted paper. Allow
to dry overnight. Check the inside
circumference of the circle and buy
the mirror cut to fit your
measurements.

   Glue the gems to the mirror
frame at regular intervals and secure
with masking tape while they dry.

4 Apply two coats of white emulsion paint to the piece, allowing the first coat to dry before applying the second. When this is dry, draw on the design for the decoration with a pencil.

5 The decoration is shown here in four stages: drawing, underpainting, overpainting, black ink outlining. Allow to dry between all paint layers, and finally allow to dry overnight before applying one coat of gloss varnish.

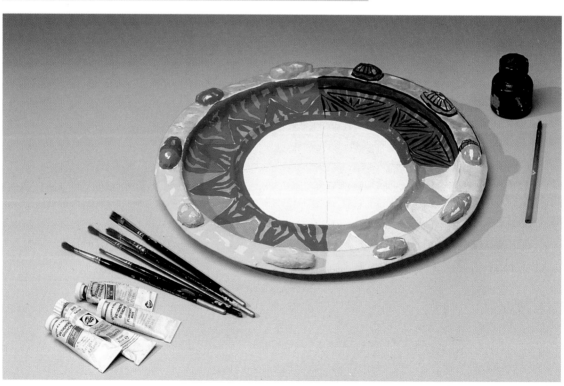

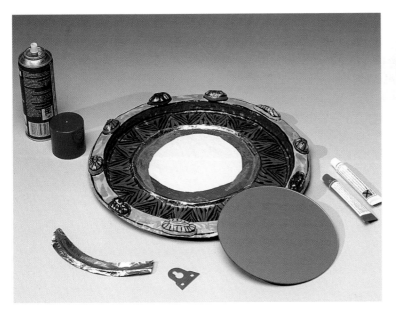

6 Cut up some strips of gold foil into curves to cover the ridge and mould it around the shape. Glue in position.

Apply a second coat of varnish over the whole piece and allow to dry before glueing the mirror to the frame and the hanger to the back.

Ensure that the clip is securely glued to the back of the mirror frame before hanging the mirror on the wall.

7 Make sure the hanger is securely glued, before hanging on the wall.

DECORATED BOX

MARION ELLIOT

THIS COLOURFUL BOX, topped with an amusing bird that forms the handle, can be used to store jewellery, sewing things, postcards or other treasures. The card construction is quite simple: the ridge on the underside of the lid holds it lightly in place without making a tight fit; the bird and the hemispheres are created from modelling plastic.

Instead of constructing a box, you could cover an old card or wooden box and give it new life. Apply two or three layers of paper pieces and follow the instructions given here for the three-dimensional and painted decoration.

Height: 16cm (6½in)

~

MATERIALS AND EQUIPMENT

- *corrugated cardboard, a piece about 38cm (15in) square* - *craft knife and scissors* - *PVA wood glue* - *masking tape* - *gummed paper tape* - *newspaper strips* - *bowl for paste* - *wallpaper paste mixed* - *modelling plastic* - *petroleum jelly* - *white emulsion paint* - *pencil or felt tip pen* - *gouache paint in various colours* - *black waterproof indian ink* - *polyurethane varnish* - *brushes: household brushes for emulsion and varnish; artists' brushes for gouache* · · · · ·

TECHNIQUES

Glue the card pieces together with PVA wood glue and hold fast with masking tape while drying for about 24 hours. Remove the masking tape and secure the joins with gummed paper tape. Also use PVA wood glue to stick the bird together and to stick the hemispheres and the bird to the box. Stick the two halves of the bird together as soon as you have removed them from the mould to prevent them from warping.

Paper one surface at a time with 2.5cm (1in) overlap onto adjoining surfaces. Apply the layers at alternating angles.

When painting the box, keep the two sections apart, and the inside can be decorated with a plain colour.

These templates show the shapes that you need to cut from cardboard in order to make this project.

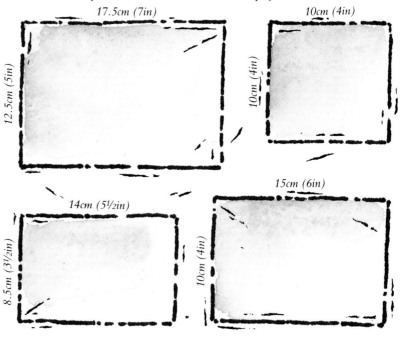

1 Cut the pieces for the box from smooth corrugated cardboard. You will need two pieces 17.5 × 12.5cm (7 × 5in) for the lid and base, two pieces 15 × 10cm (6 × 4in) for the long sides, two pieces 10 × 10cm (4 × 4in) for the short sides, one piece 14 × 8.5cm (5½ × 3½in) for the inside rim of the lid.

Seal all the pieces with diluted PVA and allow to dry before assembly.

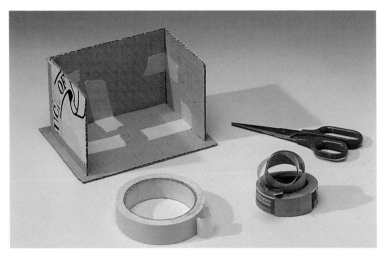

2 Assemble the box, as follows. Glue one long side in position on the base 1cm (⅜in) from the edge and hold in place with masking tape on both sides while drying. Glue the short sides, and then the other long side. When dry, remove the masking tape and secure the joins with gummed paper tape.

3 Glue the rim centrally onto the lid, secure with gummed paper tape and cover with three layers of pasted newspaper strips, with the layers at alternating angles. Apply three layers of pasted paper to the base of the box. Allow to dry for two days.

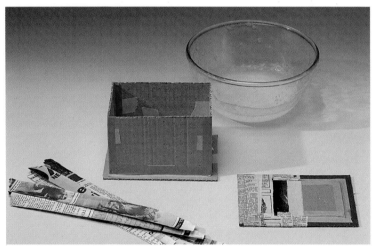

4 Shape the moulds for the balls and the bird in modelling plastic with your fingers. Cover with petroleum jelly and apply five layers of pasted newspaper to the moulds. Allow to dry for two days.

5 Cut in equal halves through the shapes and remove the moulds. Glue the two halves of the bird back together and cover the join with small strips of pasted paper.

6 Glue the hemispheres and the bird to the lid of the box and secure with masking tape while drying.

Glue the hemispheres to the base in the same way.

Apply a layer of small paper strips to smooth the joins between the box and the additional pieces, and allow to dry.

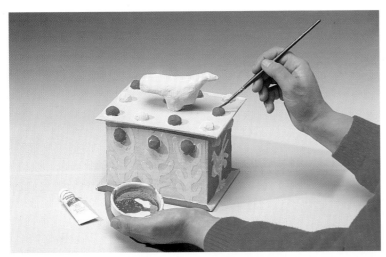

7 Apply two coats of emulsion to the inside and outside of the lid and the base, allowing drying time for each. When dry draw on the design and do the broad underpainting, then the overpainting, and then the black outlining and detail with ink, again allowing drying time between each stage.

8 The completed base and lid are finished with three coats of varnish before fitting the two together.

CAT MASK

MARION ELLIOT

This smiling cat, with its startled eyes, alert ears and flaring nostrils is influenced by the distinctive style of the Balinese spirit masks. If you want to create your own design, you could look at other animals to give you inspiration.

The mask is designed to be hung from the wall, but it is light enough to be worn. If you are going to wear it, you will have to adapt the measurements for the design to suit your own face and cut holes for eyes.

This project demands a certain amount of sculpturing skill with modelling plastic to provide the mould, but don't let this put you off. The drawing gives you the guidelines for proportion and outlines, and the modelling stage is shown in two colours to help you to see how the features are built up.

Height: 30cm (1ft); Width 16cm (6½in)

~

MATERIALS

* paper, pencil, ruler, and piece of string for measuring and drawing the design
* modelling plastic: about 2kg (4¼lbs)
* newspaper torn into strips about 2.5cm (1in) wide of various lengths
* bowl for paste
* mixed quantity of wallpaper paste
* scissors
* scalpel
* cotton wool
* white emulsion paint
* gouache paints
* black waterproof Indian ink
* polyurethane gloss varnish
* brushes: household brushes for emulsion and varnish, artists' brushes for gouache and ink
* panel pin, small hammer and darning needle or small hand drill
* galvanized steel wire for whiskers, 61cm (2ft) long cut into 6 equal lengths
* pliers
* round black elastic, 30cm (1ft) long

. . . . .

TECHNIQUES

To adapt the design for your own use as a mask take measurements from your own face to determine the length and width (from the top of your forehead to chin and from ear to ear), and the relative position of your eyes, nose and mouth. Measure with a ruler or a piece of string, following the contours of your face and then transfer these onto a piece of paper and plot out the position of the features and adapt the drawing.

The holes for the elastic should be at least 1.5cm (½in) from the edge of the mask and just above where your ears will be.

The whiskers are rather sharp, so are best omitted if you are going to wear the mask.

When using modelling plastic, work on a surface that will not stick to it. It may help you to place the drawing over the modelling material and trace the features through, using a ball point pen to define the areas.

If you are going to wear the mask, you do not need to model the eyes, just leave them flat.

Papering the mould is fiddly work, as there are so many different shapes to encounter, but make sure that you cover the mask evenly with eight layers. You will need to tear the paper into very small pieces to get into corners. Using alternate layers of paper of different colours will help you. Smooth down the paper to remove excess paste and air bubbles on the completion of each layer.

Allow the papier mâché to dry for four days in a warm airy place. Use a blunt knife to prize away the sides. Continue only if it comes away easily, otherwise allow to dry for a further day. Once out of the mould, allow a further day of drying before continuing.

Apply three coats of varnish in all, two before you pierce the holes for the whiskers and elastic, and one afterwards.

Draw the outline of the mask roughly in pencil until you are happy with its shape. Then ink it in and scale it up to the required size.

1 If you are going to hang the mask from the wall, you can work from the drawing illustrated by enlarging it on a photocopier to a height of 30cm (1ft) and a width of 16cm (6½in), or by scaling up the drawing on a grid. If you want to wear the mask, follow the instructions given in the Techniques introduction.

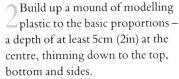Build up a mound of modelling plastic to the basic proportions – a depth of at least 5cm (2in) at the centre, thinning down to the top, bottom and sides.

Model the features with your hands, cutting away and adding where necessary. Add raised features with balls and coiled rolls of modelling plastic and build up the features to a height of about 10cm (4in) at the highest points (such as the nose). When you are happy with your work, coat the modelling plastic liberally with petroleum jelly.

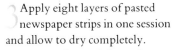Apply eight layers of pasted newspaper strips in one session and allow to dry completely.

Remove the mask from the mould and trim with scissors around the edge. Bind the edges with a layer of small pieces of pasted paper.

(If you are going to wear the mask, cut out the holes for the eyes using a scalpel, and then bind the edges with a layer of small paper strips.)

Leave the binding edges to dry before smoothing the outside and inside surface of the mask, using medium and then fine grade sandpaper.

4 Remove the excess petroleum jelly with cotton wool and white spirit to allow the surface to accept the paint on the inside of the mask. Apply two coats of white emulsion paint on both sides, allowing the first to dry before applying the second.

Draw the details of the design onto the mask in pencil.

5 Do the underpainting, and when dry, apply further layers of colour. Paint the detailed features on the mask with black waterproof indian ink. Paint the inside of the mask, too, in an appropriate colour.

When dry, apply two coats of gloss varnish, allowing the first to dry before applying the second.

6 To pierce holes for the elastic and for the whiskers carefully tap a panel pin into the inside of the mask using a small hammer. When you have started to make a hole, carefully work at it with a darning needle. (Alternatively, use a small bit and a hand drill if you have one.)

Touch up the small exposed areas of the paper with paint. When dry apply a third coat of varnish.

Thread the elastic through the holes from the outside and knot securely on the inside.

For the whiskers, use pliers to make a knot at one end of each piece of wire and thread through from the inside fastening the knot to the inside with insulating tape.

7 Bend the whisker wire with your fingers or with pliers into a zig-zag pattern for the final effect.

ARTICULATED DOLL

DEBORAH SCHNEEBELI-MORRELL

THIS EARTHY little character is directly inspired by the traditional papier mâché dolls made today by peasants in Mexico. The artist has recreated the freshness of the design and the decoration, but has made certain modifications in employing more sophisticated techniques. Whereas the Mexicans use string to join the limbs and the body, elastic is used here to give better articulation. The richness of the mixed raw pigments of the originals has been imitated by using strong acrylic paints. A protective coat of matt varnish seals the painted surface and can be wiped clean, so the doll can be handled and played with.

You could make a whole family in a range of different sizes, and a doll made to a height of 15cm (6in) would be in scale with the Doll's House project.

Height: 26cm (10in)

~

MATERIALS

● *modelling plastic: 1kg
(2lbs)* ● *newspaper torn into
5cm (2in) square pieces*
● *bowl for paste* ● *mixed
quantity of wallpaper paste
with PVA added* ● *scalpel*
● *PVA wood glue* ● *masking
tape* ● *ready-mixed acrylic
gesso* ● *acrylic paint* ● *acrylic
matt varnish* ● *brushes:
medium-sized artists' brushes
for gesso, varnish, and
painting base colour; smaller
artists' brushes for detail
painting* ● *heavy duty black
shirring elastic, 45cm (18in)
long* ● *upholsterer's mattress
needle or long darning needle*
. . . . . .

TECHNIQUES

*It is advisable to smear petroleum jelly
over the mould, though this is not
essential since modelling plastic has its
own natural grease, and the paper can
be removed quite easily from small
pieces such as these.*

*The mould can be reused if you
remove the paper shell carefully, and
smooth over the cut marks left by the
knife.*

*Add a small quantity of PVA to the
paste to give it extra adhesion.*

*Use paper of two different colours so
that you can count the layers and give
an even coverage. Wipe the paste onto
both sides of the paper and arrange
several pieces around the rim of the
bowl to soak up the glue for a few
minutes before applying. Apply six
layers in one session and allow to dry
for two days, or overnight in an airing
cupboard.*

*After removing the shells of papier
mâché from the moulds, stick the two
halves of each piece together with PVA
wood glue as soon as you have cut them
or some shrinkage may occur and the fit
will not be so neat.*

1 Model the pieces for the mould
in modelling plastic with your
hands. Make the head and body in
one piece, and left and right legs
and arms. The head and body are
17cm (6½in) long, the arms 9cm
(3½in), the legs 11cm (4½in).

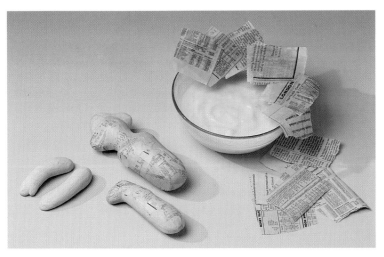

2 Apply six layers of pasted newspaper pieces, tearing them into smaller pieces where necessary to create a really smooth surface. Leave to dry for two days.

3 To free the mould from the paper, cut with a scalpel well into the modelling plastic around the sides of the body and the limbs.

4 Gently peel the paper shape from the modelling plastic. If you want to re-use the moulds, smooth over the cuts with your fingers.

5 Stick the two halves of the limbs and body together and wipe off any excess glue. Secure with strips of masking tape while the glue dries.

When the glue has set, remove the masking tape and cover the join with two layers of tiny strips of pasted newspaper. Leave to dry.

6 Apply four even coats of gesso, allowing each coat to dry before applying the next.

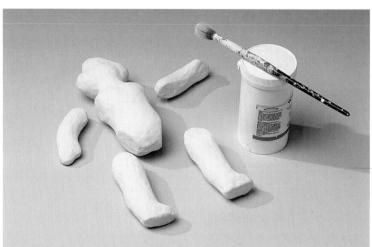

7 Apply the paint. Brush on the base areas of colour, and when dry, add the decorative details and the facial features. The white areas are not painted.

When dry, apply a coat of varnish.

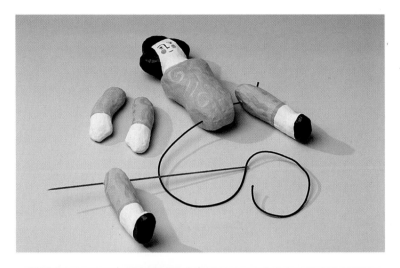

8 Assemble the doll by threading a piece of elastic straight through the limbs and the body from one side to the other, using an upholsterer's mattress needle or a long darning needle.

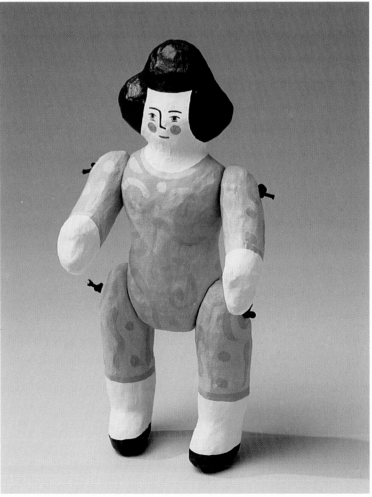

9 Secure with a knot on both sides of the shoulders and hips, allowing some movement of the pieces without stress. Put a dot of glue on the ends of the elastic to prevent it from fraying.

DOLL'S HOUSE FURNITURE

DEBORAH SCHNEEBELI-MORRELL

Doll's house furniture is expensive to buy, and yet so easy to make using inexpensive materials. Draw your inspiration from furniture around you and from photographs in magazines, simplify the designs and work out the pieces you need, bearing in mind the scale in relation to your doll's house.

The instructions given on the following pages for the basic method of construction of the dresser can be applied to all the pieces shown in the Doll's House project on page 90 (although the four-poster bed has the additional feature of small wooden posts).

It is in the painting that the pieces really come alive. Use vibrant colours, and apply the decoration spontaneously without preliminary drawing.

Height of dresser: 18cm (7in)

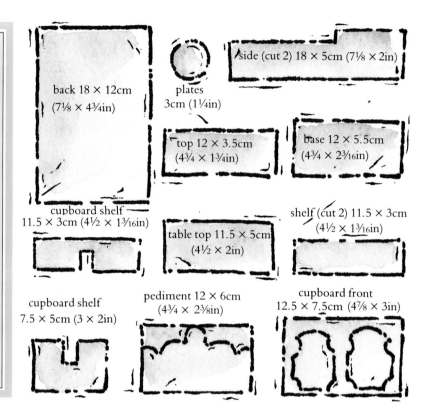

back 18 × 12cm (7⅛ × 4¾in)

plates 3cm (1¼in)

side (cut 2) 18 × 5cm (7⅛ × 2in)

top 12 × 3.5cm (4¾ × 1¼in)

base 12 × 5.5cm (4¾ × 2³⁄₁₆in)

cupboard shelf 11.5 × 3cm (4½ × 1³⁄₁₆in)

table top 11.5 × 5cm (4½ × 2in)

shelf (cut 2) 11.5 × 3cm (4½ × 1³⁄₁₆in)

cupboard shelf 7.5 × 5cm (3 × 2in)

pediment 12 × 6cm (4¾ × 2⅜in)

cupboard front 12.5 × 7.5cm (4⅞ × 3in)

MATERIALS

- corrugated card, a single piece 27 × 50cm (10½in × 1ft 8in) • mounting board, a single piece 10 × 20cm (4 × 8in) • craft knife • cutting mat • pencil or pen • steel ruler • PVA wood glue • masking tape • newspaper torn into pieces about 1.5 × 8cm (½ × 3in) • bowl for paste • wallpaper paste with small quantity of PVA added • ready-mixed acrylic gesso • acrylic paint • acrylic matt varnish • brushes: medium-sized artists' brushes for gesso and varnish; finer artists' brushes for paint
. . . . . .

TECHNIQUES

The width of the card you use will affect the measurements when working on such a small scale, so you may have to do some trimming to adjust the fit if you use card of a different thickness than used here (2mm/⅛in). Cut out the base, sides and back first and assemble, and then check for fit before cutting out the other pieces. Use PVA wood glue and stick the pieces together in the correct order. Hold the pieces fast with masking tape while the glue dries.

Add a small quantity of PVA to the wallpaper paste mixture to give it extra strength. Wipe the paste on both sides of the paper and arrange several pieces around the edge of the paste bowl for a few minutes before using. Apply two layers of pasted paper to the dresser in one session and allow to dry for two days.

1 Draw out the plan of the pieces needed on a piece of corrugated card and cut out, using a craft knife and a metal straight edge on a cutting mat.

Mark out nine circles from mounting board and cut out.

2 Assemble the dresser, starting with the back and the sides. Then glue on the base, the top, the table top and the two shelves (f&g). Slot together the cupboard shelves and glue in position. Cut out the detailing of the cupboard front and the pediment and glue on.

Cut thin slivers of mounting card to form the tiny ridges for the shelves and stick in position.

Use small pieces of masking tape to hold it together while the glue is drying so that it keeps its shape.

3 Remove the tape. Apply two layers of pasted paper strips to all the visible surfaces of the dresser, tearing the paper into tiny pieces to fit the shapes including the front of the shelves, and leave the back uncovered.

4 Allow to dry for two days, and then coat with four layers of gesso, allowing each to dry out completely before applying the next.

Coat the plates with four layers of gesso.

5 When dry, paint the inside back and sides of the dresser with yellow paint. Paint two tones of the blue-grey decoration on the front and the plates.

When dry, apply a coat of matt varnish.

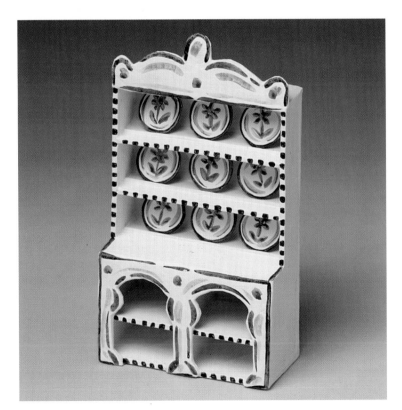

6 Apply a small dot of glue to the top of the back of the plates and carefully stick them in position behind the ridge on the shelves.

The construction of the different pieces of furniture on page 88 follows essentially the same method as that given here for the dresser.

DOLL'S HOUSE

DEBORAH SCHNEEBELI-MORRELL

DOLL'S HOUSES hold a fascination for both adults and children alike, and though traditionally made of wood, the strong card construction of this papier mâché doll's house will stand up to normal use as well as being highly decorative.

It shows a magical juxtaposition of styles: the exterior is a wedding cake fantasy, derived from a classic Georgian-style vicarage, with an elaborate decorative pediment inspired by Mexican Baroque churches; the interior, in contrast to the serene exterior, reveals a riot of wild and dynamic colour, again inspired by Mexican themes. The papier mâché furniture inside is also eclectic in its design, full of imagination – there is even a miniature papier mâché doll's house on the table.

The construction requires precise working, and the measurements in metric are those used by the designer. Tackled logically it is quite easy to follow. See page 86 for instructions for making the dresser, and page 80 for a doll similar to the one shown here.

Height: 88cm (2ft 11in)

~

MATERIALS

● *large quantity double strength corrugated card (discarded uncreased packing boxes are useful)* ● *corrugated card with single corrugations for pilasters, and for door and window templates* ● *pencil or pen* ● *metal straight edge for cutting against* ● *craft knife* ● *strong PVA waterproof wood glue* ● *masking tape* ● *heavy weights (several large books)* ● *strong artists' canvas: cut 2 strips, 54.5 × 7cm (21½ × 2¾in)* ● *scissors* ● *bowl for paste* ● *newspaper torn into pieces of various sizes* ● *wallpaper paste with addition of PVA* ● *paper pulp* ● *ready-prepared decorators' filler* ● *ready-prepared acrylic gesso* ● *acrylic paints* ● *water pot and palette* ● *acrylic matt varnish* ● *brushes: medium-sized artists' brushes for gesso, paint, and varnish; small artists' brushes for painting detailed decoration*

. . . . . .

TECHNIQUES

The main pieces of the doll's house are made from two layers of double-corrugated card. The two layers of card should be glued together (with the smoothest sides outermost) before the pieces are cut out. Spread a liberal amount of strong PVA wood glue evenly over the surface of one piece and weight the two sheets together until dry.

The measurements given in the diagrams are based on the double layer of card having a thickness of 1.5cm (⅝in). If using card of a different thickness you will have to adjust the measurements. It is important to cut and assemble the pieces in the order shown so that you can check the fit as you go along.

Use a craft knife and a metal straight edge to cut the pieces, glue together with PVA glue and hold them fast with masking tape until they have dried.

The ground paper pulp should be mixed according to the maker's instructions, and then add some ready-prepared decorators' filler for additional strength and to prevent shrinkage.

You will need a large quantity of paste with a generous quantity of PVA glue added to give additional adhesion.

Smooth the paper down very flat to ensure maximum contact between the paper and the card. Work carefully around the decorative areas modelled with pulp, tearing the paper into tiny pieces to avoid creases. Paper both sides of the card in one session to prevent warping.

Some warping will be unavoidable, and it will add character, but when drying the doors especially, be sure to weight them down to ensure that they fit. (It is also advisable to place the doors in position in the house between working sessions to prevent fitting problems.)

The canvas hinges are glued to the door and the side of the door frame with PVA glue. Apply glue to both the canvas and to the card.

CUT FROM TWO SHEETS OF PREPARED DOUBLE-CORRUGATED CARD

Base
Top: 73 × 31cm (28¾ × 12¼in)
Front: 73 × 13cm (28¾ × 5in)
Sides: 28 × 13cm (11 × 5in)
(cut two pieces)
Back: 73 × 13cm (28¾ × 5in)

Pediment
Front: 71 × 21cm (28 × 8¼in)
Reinforcement pieces: 71 × 4cm (28 × 1½in) (cut two pieces)

Main shell
Back: 68 × 55cm (26¾ × 21½in)
Sides: 55 × 26.5cm (21½ × 10½in) (cut two pieces)
Top: 68 × 25cm (26¾ × 10in)
Bottom: 68 × 25cm (26¾ × 10in)

Interior
Dividing walls: 25.25 × 25cm (10 × 10in) (cut four pieces)
First floor: 68 × 25cm (26¾ × 10in)

Doors
Cut one 70.5 × 54.5cm (27¾ × 21½in) then cut vertically along one-third interval (to make two pieces, one 47cm (18½in) wide, and one 23.5cm (9¼in) wide)

CUT FROM ONE LAYER OF SINGLE-CORRUGATED CARD

Template for windows: 9.5 × 12cm (3¾ × 4¾in)
Template for door: 9.5 × 17cm (3¾ × 6¾in)

Pilasters
Vertical pieces for door: 54.5 × 3cm (27¾ × 1¼in) (cut four pieces)
Vertical pieces for sides: 55 × 3cm (27¾ × 1¼in) (cut four pieces)
Horizontal pieces for door and sides should be cut to fit

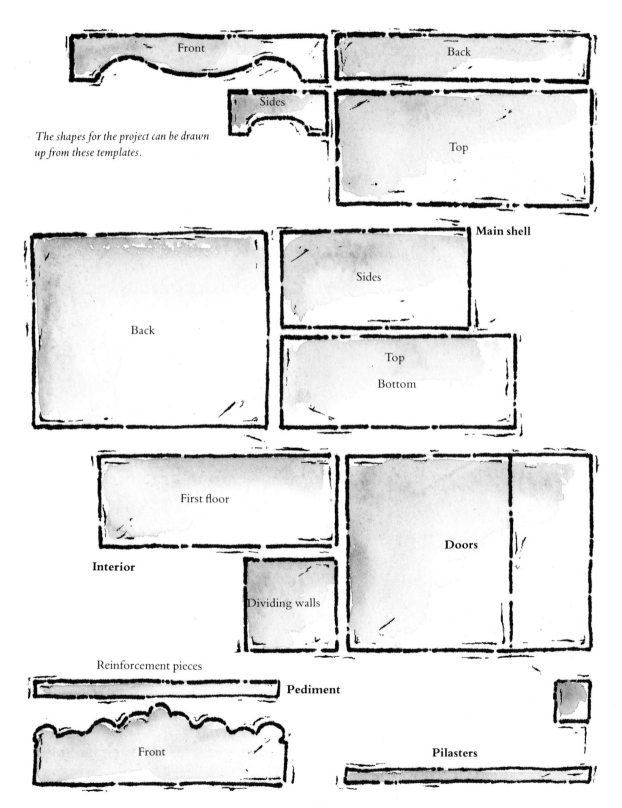

Front

Back

Sides

The shapes for the project can be drawn up from these templates.

Top

Main shell

Back

Sides

Top

Bottom

First floor

Doors

Interior

Dividing walls

Reinforcement pieces

Pediment

Front

Pilasters

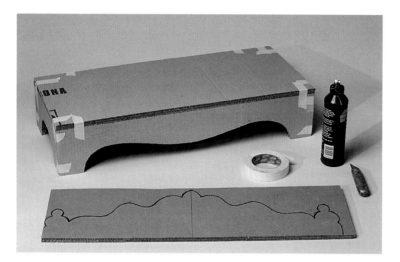

1 Cut out the pieces for the base and assemble, laying the top of the base on the work surface and constructing it upside down. Glue the front and back to the top first, and then the sides.

Draw the outline for the pediment (scale up the template, or draw one half by eye and reverse the outline for the other half). Cut. out as carefully as possible with a craft knife.

Cut out the reinforcing strips and glue them together (making four layers of card). Glue to the back of the base of the pediment.

2 Assemble the main shell of the house. Glue the back to one side, then attach the bottom, then the top, then the other side. Tape securely in position while the glue dries.

Stick the main shell to the base, allowing more of the base to protrude at the front to accommodate the thickness of the doors, and an even amount to show around the sides and back.

Cut out the first floor piece and the dividing walls and glue in place.

3 Cut out the piece for the door (it should be 0.5cm (¼in) shorter than the height of the sides of the house to avoid fitting problems), then cut the opening along one third of its width.

Stick the pediment to the top of the house, leaving it proud at the front by the thickness of the doors so that they will be flush when closed.

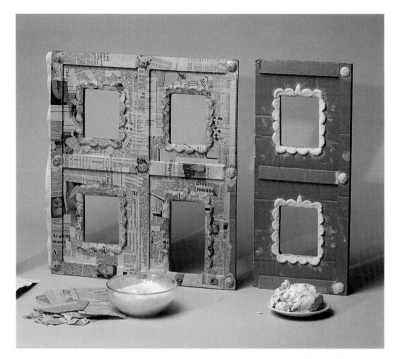

4 Cut the pilaster strips for the sides and glue as shown, leaving a gap of 3cm (⅝in) at the front edges where the canvas hinges will be stuck.

Cut the pilaster strips for the doors. The vertical pilaster on the joining edge of the larger door projects by 1.5cm (½in) and a corresponding gap should be left on the edge of the other door so that they close neatly.

Cut out a template for the windows and the door, mark their positions by eye and cut out the shapes.

Model the window frames, the door surround and the roundels on the pilasters with paper pulp and allow to dry overnight.

5 Cover the doors with two layers of pasted paper, leaving a 3cm (1¼in) gap on the outside edges of the back for the canvas hinge. Work the back and front of the doors in one session to prevent warping. Allow to dry for 24 hours, weighting them down to prevent them from warping.

Stick the canvas hinges to the back of both doors, making sure that you cover both sides of the canvas with glue to ensure a strong join. Apply two layers of paper over the canvas up to the edge of the door.

6 Model the pulp decoratively over the pediment area and allow to dry.

Paper the whole doll's house (except the strip on the front edge of the sides where the hinge will be attached) with two layers and allow to dry for 24 hours.

7 Glue the hinges to the front edges of the sides and allow to dry.

Glue the pilasters over the canvas strips on the sides and then paper over the cardboard with two layers of paper and allow to dry.

8 Give the whole doll's house four layers of gesso, avoiding the canvas hinge, allowing each layer to dry before applying the next.

9 Finally, you can decorate the house. Here, acrylic paints are used, the areas decorated with pulp are left white and the shapes are picked out with dark and light tones of blue–black paint. The colours of the rooms are varied, and a patterned border is given to the front edges.

Once the paint is dry, apply a coat of acrylic matt varnish.

INDEX

INDEX